Maths Around Us

Using Subtraction at the Park

Tracey Steffora

www.raintreepublishers.co.uk
Visit our website to find out more information about Raintree books.

To order:

☎ Phone 0845 6044371

🖹 Fax +44 (0) 1865 312263

🖥 Email myorders@raintreepublishers.co.uk

Customers from outside the UK please telephone +44 1865 312262

Edited by Rebecca Rissman, Tracey Steffora, and Catherine Veitch
Designed by Joanna Hinton-Malivoire
Picture research by Elizabeth Alexander
Production by Victoria Fitzgerald
Originated by Capstone Global Library Ltd
Printed and bound in China by Leo Paper Products Ltd

ISBN 978 1 406 22318 7
15 14 13 12 11
10 9 8 7 6 5 4 3 2 1

British Library Cataloguing in Publication Data
Steffora, Tracey.
Using subtraction at the park. -- (Maths around us)
513.2'12-dc22

Acknowledgements
The author and publisher are grateful to the following for permission to reproduce photographs: © Capstone Publishers pp. 18, 19, 20 (Karon Dubke); Alamy pp. 4 (© PCL), 5 (© Gregory Wrona), 6 (© Andy Salter), 10 (© Tracey Foster), 22 (Paul Springett 02); Corbis p. 14 (© moodboard); Shutterstock pp. 7 (© Paula Cobleigh), 9 (© Manamana), 11 (© Mircea Bezergheanu), 13 (© Kheng Guan Toh), 15 (© c.), 15 (© marre), 15 background (© val lawless), 16 (© c.), 16 (© marre), 16 background (© val lawless), 21 (© David P. Lewis), 23 glossary – marble (© marre), 23 glossary – squirrel (© Paula Cobleigh), 23 glossary – swan (© Kheng Guan Toh).

Cover photograph of children playing hide-and-seek in the park reproduced with permission of Photolibrary (Juice Images). Back cover photograph of a grey squirrel reproduced with permission of Shutterstock (© Paula Cobleigh).

We would like to thank Nancy Harris, Dee Reid, and Diana Bentley for their assistance in the preparation of this book.

Every effort has been made to contact copyright holders of material reproduced in this book. Any omissions will be rectified in subsequent printings if notice is given to the publisher.

Contents

At the park

A park is a busy place.

People come and go at the park.

Animals come and go at the park.

Take one away

There are two squirrels on the grass.

One squirrel runs up a tree.
How many are left?

Start with two. Take one away.

There is one squirrel left.

Take two away

There are four swans in the water.

Two swans fly away.
How many are left?

Start with four. Take two away.

There are two swans left.

Take three away

Some children are playing marbles.

How many marbles are in this circle?
What if three are hit out of the circle?

Start with six. Take three away.

Six take away three equals three.

$$6 - 3 = 3$$

There are three marbles left.

Three children are on the swings.

All three children leave.

How many children are left?

3 − 3 = 0

There are no children left on the swings.

It is time to go home. Tomorrow will
be another day at the park!

Subtraction story

Look at the picture. Can you write your own subtraction story?

Picture glossary

 **marble** small glass ball used to play games

 **squirrel** animal that has a bushy tail and strong back legs

 **swan** large water bird with a long neck